Copyright November 3, 2010 Bill Wagenheim

Published by: Smart Money Management

Bill Wagenheim
574 Delaware Avenue
Delmar, NY 12054
518-439-2190

All rights reserved. No part of this manual may be reproduced, stored in a retrieval system or transmitted in any form or by any means, electronic, mechanical, photo copying, recording, or otherwise, without the prior permission of Smart Money Management.

Manufactured in the United States of America

This Certificate issued under the seal of the CopyrightOffice in accordance with title 17, *United States Code,* attest that registration has been made for the work identified below. The information on this certificate has been made a part of the Copyright Office records.

Marian A. Pallante
Acting Register of Copyrights, United States of America

Registration Number
TXu 1-709-113

Effective date of registration: November 3, 2010

Title of Work: You can be...Debt Free
Completion/Publication
Year of Completion: 2004
ISBN: 978-0-692-01265-9

Contents

Genesis i
Mission & Purpose ii

SECTION 1

Fast Track Cash Flow Expense and Debt Worksheet 1
Worksheet Illustration: Fast Track Cash Flow Expense and Debt Worksheet   2
Worksheet Illustration: Fast Track Cash Flow Expense and Debt Worksheet Completed   2-1
Setting up the Account Schedule and Monthly Allocation from Your Worksheet: Expenses 3
Worksheet Illustration: Setting up the Account Schedule and Monthly Allocation – Expenses   4
Worksheet: Account Schedule Blank Form   4-1
Worksheet: Account Schedule Blank Form   4-2

Setting up the Account Schedule and Monthly Allocation from Your Worksheet: Debts 5
Worksheet Illustration: Setting up the Account Schedule and Monthly Allocation - Debts   6

Adjust Expense Estimate to Actual Bill 7
Transaction Record Guidelines for Entries in our System and your Checkbook Register   7
Worksheet Illustration: Adjust Expense Estimate to Actual Bill   8

Highlight Paid Bills: Taking Control of Timely Payments 9
Worksheet Illustration: Take Control: Pay Bills on Time   10

January's Account Schedule and Monthly Allocation 11
Change Your Life Style: Meet Freddy Frugal   11
The PCF Formula   11
-Worksheet Illustration: January's Allocation Schedule and Monthly Allocation -
Action Column: % -$. TIA: Take Immediate Action to Reduce Debt and Interest Expense   12

SECTION 2

Transaction Record is the same as your Checkbook Register, Plus Cash Cushion 13
Adjust Expense Estimate in Cash Cushion Column   13
January's Transaction Record Balanced. Bring Balance Forward to February   13
Worksheet Illustration: Transaction Record is the same as your Checkbook Register + Cash Cushion – Adjust expense estimate in Cash Cushion Column   14
Worksheet Illustration: January's Transaction Record Balanced – Bring Balance Forward to February   15
Worksheet: Transaction Record Blank Form   15-1
Start Next Month's Account Schedule – February 16
February's Completed Account Schedule   16
Worksheet Illustration: February's Account Schedule: Debt and Finance Charges Reduced – Savings Increased   17

Transaction Record Guidelines for Credit Card Charges 18
Debt Management is not a Science   18
Simple vs. Complex   18
Balance Transaction Record and Credit Card Charge Balance   18

Contents Continued on Next Page

Contents (continued)

Transaction Record guidelines for Credit Card Charges (Continued) 18
Worksheet Illustration: Transaction Record guidelines for Credit Card Charges   19
                 Credit Card Charges Column List Credit Charges   19
                 Credit Card Charge Balance Column add (+) each Charge to Balance   19
                 Deduct (-) Credit Card Charges from Balance   19
Worksheet Illustration: Balancing Transaction Record and Credit Card Charge Balance   20

SECTION 3

Learn the Best Kept Secret: the Power of Compound Interest 21
Compounding Debt Payments   21
The High Cost of Single Debt Reduction Payments   21
Chart: Summary of Payment Methods: Single Debt Reduction vs. Compounded Payments   21

Hammer Debts – Accelerated Debt Payment Plan = Compounding 22
Chart   22

Bill Paying Process – Master the Paper Trail. 23
The Envelope: Debit/Credit Card Receipts   23
Balance your Checkbook   23

SECTION 4

The American Dream Part 1 24
The Bridge Between Substance (financial security) and Your Life Style   24

The American Dream Part 2 25

SECTION 5

Wealth Accumulation 26
Chart   26

Genesis

I thank my ex business partner, Albert Stone for the genesis of Debt Free. Without realizing it, this system evolved from Al's PCF – Positive Cash Flow analysis, a business we owned many years ago.

After I retired from business, I accumulated large debt because of major health problems in my family, my own failure to curb credit card and equity loan debt, a new home, furniture, landscaping, Florida winter vacations, and on and on. I had lost financial control. I always had good organizational skills, but I still couldn't find a way to reduce debt. I started with budgets, writing down all my purchases. But when I looked at all my cash expenditures, movies, groceries, ATM withdrawals, and dozens of other items, with little pieces of paper stuck in my pocket to add to my five page budget list, I gave up. It was like chasing a ghost.

But ah, I remembered Al's PCF- Positive Cash Flow formula. We had a chain of furniture and appliance stores, plus a television and appliance service company. Our office staff included an accountant, bookkeeper, assistant, several office workers, plus an outside accounting firm. Neither Al nor I had any accounting background; we relied on our staff and accounting firm for guidance in supporting the financial end of our business.

There were stacks of computer reports: inventory, accounts payable, sales, profit and loss statements, balance sheets, taxes, and depreciation schedules. When we sat at our conference table across from each other, all I could see was Al's bald head beyond the stacks of reports.

Our accountant prepared some of the reports, profit and loss statements, and our accounting firm completed the balance sheet and reviewed them with us. After a few monthly five hour sessions with dozens of cups of coffee, plus huge headaches and lots of Excedrin, we did digest the information. Al pored over the reams of data and extracted numbers that made sense to him. He said "If we can control expenses, increase our cash flow, and have more coming in than going out, the rest will take care of itself." And it does. Al called it PCF: Positive Cash Flow.

So, by extracting all operating expenses, measuring them by percentages month to month for increases/decreases, and monitoring sales volume, Al created a monthly analysis of our cash flow. We then acted and corrected any expense item out of line with his cash flow analysis. That process saved us thousands of dollars yearly, and with other innovative actions, we operated our business successfully as a partnership for 30 years.

Years later, finding myself in huge debt, I thought back to the years in business and applied the PCF: Positive Cash Flow formula to achieve a debt free life. I modified the concept and adapted it to educational workshops where I teach Debt Free at Community & Professional Education, Hudson Valley Community College, Troy, NY; and a private debt counseling practice. I now counsel others to a debt free life, and a start to building wealth.

Mission & Purpose

What is it that we do?
We are the architects of cash management. Unlike financial journalists, syndicated columnists, and internet financial gurus, with tips and advice on every financial subject, we concentrate our efforts on simple formulas to control spending and reduce debts. Writers of budget books with hundreds of budget categories leave us dazed, and after many failed attempts at budgeting we quit. No wonder. Credit counseling services can package a debt repayment plan at a high cost to the debtor, a high monthly fee, frozen credit and a damaged credit rating that will last for years.

We are the only ones who do what we do!

No other system of household debt management is as simple to use, and yet so effective. Our Debt Free system gives you the flexibility of cash and debit/credit card spending, while you still maintain total control of your cash. You will immediately take control of your debts by manageable debt reducing payments and the timely reminders of payment due dates.

You may not have complete knowledge of debt management or financial matters, but you can learn to be debt free, save and accumulate wealth if you concentrate on the basic formulas in our Debt Free System.

The mechanics of Debt Free is not enough. You are guided by the value *you* place on being debt free. Connect your "value system" to the Debt Free system and a debt free life.

In our workbook manual you will learn three basic steps to guide you to zero debt, with a real life example of how it's done. By starting with our simple worksheet of your recurring expenses and debts, we make our system easy to use. No budgets are required.

Here are our Three Basic Steps to Zero Debt:

Step 1 Your Personal Financial Statement
Prepare our simple no budget worksheet of your recurring expenses and debts; estimate your monthly income and Debt Free will give you a picture of your cash flow daily. Just like a business you have a profit and loss statement built in every month. You don't have to wait months to find out you're going broke.

Step 2 Positive Cash Flow Formula
Debt Free sets up a Cash Cushion after all expenses and debts have been allocated. The Cash Cushion is for daily-living life-style spending. This formula limits your spending to the amount in Cash Cushion. And no budgets are required!

Here is the Formula:

    Checking Account Balance
    +Estimated Monthly Income
    =Available Funds
     -Monthly Allocation
    =Cash Cushion

Step 3 Hammer Debts
Hammer debts to zero in half the time by compounding payments. Learn the power of compound interest. If you are on the wrong side of that compound interest, high credit card interest rates, it can take years to pay off. By accelerating debt payments, you reverse the cycle. Compounding is cutting finance charges as well as debt.

Section 1

$MART MONEY MANAGEMENT
debt proof your life...

You can be... Debt Free

> "Wealth is not the same as income. If you make a good income and spend it all, you're not getting wealthier, you are just living high. Wealth is what you accumulate, not what you spend."

Thomas J. Stanley and William D. Danko
The Millionaire Next Door

You can be... Debt Free

Fast Track Cash Flow Expense and Debt Worksheet
(worksheet illustration page 2)

Don't let this form intimidate you. The Cash Flow Expense and Debt Worksheet is the shortest distance between debt and solvency. This form is a snapshot picture of your financial condition to evaluate your cash flow. The Cash Flow schedule is a guide to help you process the Monthly Allocation. Calculate expenses that are quarterly, semi-annual or annual into monthly payments. For debt payments, compile your credit card statements; loans, enter balances, interest rates, plus the cost of debt; finance charges. Enter monthly expenses and debts.

> "Saving isn't easy. It requires discipline, knowledge, and forethought. An effective saver is able to forego the instant but short-lived gratification of spending money now. Becoming an effective saver requires knowledge about the flow of money into and out of your life, something amazingly few people know much about. Finally, effective saving requires the ability to plan ahead to avoid unpleasant and costly surprises in your financial life. Done properly, saving becomes a habit that is hard to kick. The instant gratification of making an impulse purchase is supplanted by the much more deeply satisfying comfort of being financially secure. The knowledge of how money is flowing through your life provides a sense of control unknown to people living from one pay check to another.
>
> The cost of most things that we buy is considerably higher than what the price tag says it cost. That's because each time you spend a dollar, you're simultaneously electing not to invest that dollar. And a dollar invested is almost always worth more than a dollar spent."

Douglas R. Sease
"Winning with the Market"

Section 1

$MART MONEY MANAGEMENT
debt proof your life...

You can be... **Debt Free**

Fast Track Cash Flow Expense and Debt Worksheet

Expenses Monthly *(scratch expenses that don't apply)*

$_____ Savings
_____ Rent/Mortgage *(include real estate, school tax, insurance)*
_____ Auto Insurance/Home Owner's
_____ Life Insurance
_____ Home Owner's/Renter's Insurance
_____ School Tuition
_____ Gas & Electric: *(average monthly bill)*
_____ Telephone: *(average monthly bill)*
_____ Lawn Maintenance/snow removal
_____ Water & Sewer
_____ TV Cable
_____ Automobile Gas
_____ Health/Dental Premiums: *(if you pay for it from your net take-home pay)*
_____ Garbage Removal
_____ Gym/Club Membership
_____ Home Cleaning Service
_____ Day Care Provider
_____ Alimony
_____ Child Support
$_____ Total Monthly Expenses

Debt Payments Monthly	Debt Balance	Interest %	Finance Charges
$_____ Auto Loan _____	$ _____	_____	_____
_____ School Loan _____	_____	_____	_____
_____ Home Equity Loan _____	_____	_____	_____
_____ Bank Loan _____	_____	_____	_____
_____ Finance Co. Loan _____	_____	_____	_____
_____ Personal Loan _____	_____	_____	_____
_____ Credit Card _____	_____	_____	_____
_____ Credit Card _____	_____	_____	_____
_____ Credit Card _____	_____	_____	_____
_____ Credit Card _____	_____	_____	_____
_____ Credit Card _____	_____	_____	_____
_____ Credit Card _____	_____	_____	_____
_____ Credit Card _____	_____	_____	_____
Total Monthly	Total		Total
$_____ Debt Payments	Debt... $_____		Finance Charges... $_____

Section 1

$MART MONEY MANAGEMENT
debt proof your life...

You can be... **Debt Free**

Fast Track Cash Flow – Expense and Debt Worksheet <u>Completed</u>

<u>Expenses Monthly</u> *(scratch expenses that don't apply)*

$ 100.00	Savings
1250.00	Rent/Mortgage *(include real estate, school tax, insurance)*
150.00	Auto Insurance/Home Owner's
75.00	Life Insurance
_____	Home Owner's/Renter's Insurance
_____	School Tuition
140.00	Gas & Electric: *(average monthly bill)*
75.00	Telephone: *(average monthly bill)*
_____	Lawn Maintenance/snow removal
_____	Water & Sewer
65.00	TV Cable
45.00	Automobile Gas
_____	Health/Dental Premiums: *(if you pay for it from your net take-home pay)*
_____	Garbage Removal
_____	Gym/Club Membership
_____	Home Cleaning Service
_____	Day Care Provider
_____	Alimony
_____	Child Support
$ 1900.00	Total Monthly Expenses

Debt Payments Monthly		Debt Balance	Interest %	Finance Charges
$ 350.00	Auto Loan BOA	$ 12,600.00	9.00%	$ 94.50
	School Loan _____	_____	_____	_____
250.00	Home Equity Loan City Bank	8,020.00	9.75%	65.16
	Bank Loan _____	_____	_____	_____
	Finance Co. Loan _____	_____	_____	_____
	Personal Loan _____	_____	_____	_____
100.00	Credit Card GM Mastercard	4,020.00	16.09%	56.62
75.00	Credit Card American Express	3,750.00	12.05%	39.06
50.00	Credit Card Capital One Visa	2,200.00	14.09%	27.32
50.00	Credit Card MBNA MasterCard	1,972.00	14.09%	24.49
50.00	Credit Card BOA (1) Visa	1,825.00	12.09%	19.62
100.00	Credit Card Sears	580.00	21.00%	10.15
100.00	Credit Card Macys	345.00	22.05%	6.47
$ 1125.00	Total Monthly Debt Payments Total Debt $ **35,312**			**$343.39**
$ 3025.00	Monthly Allocation (Expenses + Debts)			

Positive Cash Flow Formula:

$ 282.00		Checking Account Balance
$ 3,725.00	+	Estimated Monthly Income
$ 4,007.00	=	Available Funds
$ 3025.00	-	Monthly Allocation
$ 982.00	=	Cash Cushion

Section 1

$MART MONEY MANAGEMENT
debt proof your life...

You can be... **Debt Free**

Setting up the Account Schedule and Monthly Allocation from your Worksheets: *Expenses*
(worksheet illustration page 4)

On the blank Account Schedule work report begin your list of *recurring* expenses, starting with "savings." *You pay yourself first.* This cash savings is ready to meet any financial emergency. Continue listing all expenses. List every expense even before the bill arrives. Check back on your last two months of major expenses and average out the monthly payments. Smooth out your quarterly, semi-annual, and annual expenses into monthly payments: auto, home owners/renter's and life insurance. Call your utility provider. They can spread your average gas & electric bills over 12 months. Now you can take control of your monthly expenses. If your monthly bills are crowded between the first and tenth of the month along with your rent/mortgage, ask your creditors to spread out the payment due dates to match your income stream. Study the list of expenses. Of the many items listed, between renters/ homeowner's, you can probably eliminate a number of items not related to your living expenses.

- **Account Schedule.** Your Fast Track Cash Flow Expense and Debt Worksheet calculations are the basis for bill paying and cash control in the Account Schedule. List all recurring monthly expenses under Account Schedule.
- **Monthly Allocation.** Enter monthly expense payments from your worksheet. Estimate average monthly payments.
- **Date Due.** Schedule your monthly expense payments at least five days before the due date, giving yourself enough time to have adequate funds in your checking account.
- **Amount due.** Enter Monthly Allocation payments in Amount Due column as you receive the bills.
- **Online Electronic Bill Pay.** Bill paying can become more efficient and less tedious through the use of electronic bill pay. Go online with your bank's Internet web site and set up an account with your recurring expenses and debts. List accounts with account numbers you want to pay. You can have your bank pay the bill automatically, or notify you with a message to your e-mail address as a notice of a date due bill. Each account will list the previous monthly payment amount and date paid, plus your checking account balance. Most bills can reach the vendor in one or two days. Check your Checking Account Balance for adequate funds, and avoid the serious consequences of late payments. You can also opt for paperless statements, and download the banks electronic statement to match your checkbook register balance. This is easy to use, and saves time and money.

> *"Saving for a rainy day may not be a priority when you're buried under credit card bills. But in the long run, an emergency fund may actually help you dig out of debt and maintain a recently improved credit score. Why? Imagine an emergency hits and you don't have any savings to pay for it. Just when you've started to make a dent in your bills, you have to put that charge on your credit card. Not only could that get you right back where you started, in terms of your debt level, but it will increase your credit card use as well, thus hurting your score. By setting aside a little bit each month, you will have money to tap without resorting to plastic.*
>
> *The trade-off here is that you'll pay off your debt more slowly. Say you have $10,000 in credit card debt at a 13.99% APR. With $500 monthly payment, you'll be debt free in 23 months, having paid a total of $1470 in interest. But what if you paid $400 toward the cards and put the other $100 in a savings account? It would take you an extra seven months to be debt-free and you'll pay an additional $443 in interest. But by the time you're debt-free, you'll also have saved $3000."*

**Mary Hunt,
Founder of Debt Proof Living.com:**
Build an Emergency Fund

Section 1

$MART MONEY MANAGEMENT
debt proof your life...

You can be... **Debt Free**

Setting up the Account Schedule and Monthly Allocation from your Worksheet: *Expenses*

Monthly Allocation	Account Schedule Month Jan. Yr. _____	Date Due	Amount Due	Date Paid	Amount Paid	Deposits	Cash Cushion	Checking Acct. Bal.	% $
100.00	Savings	—	100.00						
1250.00	Citibank—mortgage	1/22	1250.00						
150.00	State Farm—auto ins.	2/9	150.00						
75.00	Met Life—insurance	1/20	75.00						
75.00	Verizon—telephone	2/8	75.00						
140.00	National Grid—elec & gas	1/19	140.00						
65.00	Time Warner—cable	1/15	65.00						
45.00	Exxon-Mobil—gas	2/4	45.00	*expenses*					

Section 1

$MART MONEY MANAGEMENT
debt proof your life...

You can be... **Debt Free**

Monthly Allocation	Account Schedule Month _____ Yr. _____	Date Due	Amount Due	Date Paid	Amount Paid	Deposits	Cash Cushion	Checking Acct. Bal.	% $

4-1

Section 1

$MART MONEY MANAGEMENT
debt proof your life...

You can be... **Debt Free**

Monthly Allocation	Account Schedule Month _____ Yr. _____	Date Due	Amount Due	Date Paid	Amount Paid	Deposits	Cash Cushion	Checking Acct. Bal.	% $
	Monthly Allocation								
	Checking Account Balance								
+	Estimated Monthly Income								
=	Available Funds								
−	Monthly Allocation								
=	Cash Cushion								

Section 1

$MART MONEY MANAGEMENT
debt proof your life...

You can be... **Debt Free**

Short in your Estimate of Monthly Income?

There can be a disruption in the flow of cash into the Checking Account Balance from an unexpected shortage in the Estimated Monthly Income. What can you do?

- Cut back on discretionary spending.
- Eliminate savings for the month.
- Draw down from savings account.
- If you use plastic and over-draw your Cash Cushion, it can set you back into a costly habit.
- If the situation is chronic, plan for part-time income.
- See Freddy Frugal page 11.
- Don't forfeit your future: debt prevents saving and investing.

This is a Checks and Balances System.

In accounting practice it is called cash basis accounting: lists income when received and expense when paid. Small businesses use this method of accounting. A monthly profit and loss statement will show a positive or negative cash flow. You strive for PCF: Positive Cash Flow, more money coming in than going out. If you want to stay financially healthy between debit and credit spending, don't exceed Cash Cushion.

Setting up the Account Schedule and Monthly Allocation from your Worksheets: *Debts* (worksheet illustration page 6)

- The cash flow expense and debt worksheet is a household debt management tool, a profit and loss statement, similar to that of any small business. It gives you a picture of your financial condition.
- **Setting up a Cash Cushion.** When you estimate credit card payments, adjust or modify payments to leave enough cash for one month's daily-living life-style spending, such as food, entertainment and other miscellaneous expenditures. Cash Cushion provides unbudgeted cash through debit card and ATM use. It is designed to limit spending. *If you are making minimum credit card payments in order to make enough for Cash Cushion spending, go to Freddy Frugal for additional help.* Adjust your spending habits. Change your life style. (Page 11 side bar)
- **Account Schedule: Listing Debts.** When listing debts, start with the largest balance, then process down to the smallest debt balance. Use your worksheet as a guide; enter debt payments, interest rates and finance charges. Each debt has an interest rate posted in the % column. Under the $ sign are the amounts of finance charges. TIA: Take Immediate Action to lower debt, and reduce finance charges. Call your credit card providers and negotiate a lower rate.
- **Monthly Allocation Formula.** This formula is the foundation for cash control and debt reduction. When you completed the Cash Flow Expense and Debt Worksheet, it gave you a picture of your financial condition. The Monthly Allocation defines the **PCF: Positive Cash Flow Formula:**

    282.00 **Checking Account Balance**
  +3725.00 **Estimated Monthly Income**
  =4007.00 **Available funds**
  -3025.00 **Monthly Allocation**
  = 982.00 **Cash Cushion**

- **Amount Due Column.** This is *not* the monthly amount due, but the total amount owed. The figures in red are the amounts of each debt. The figures in black are monthly expenses. View items in black as overhead, home operating expenses. The figures in red $35,312 are all debt.
- **Debt to Income Ratio.** By dividing $1125.00, the monthly payments to cover debt, by $3725.00 net monthly income, we arrive at the percentage of debt = to 30.26. Money Management International, a non-profit consumer counseling organization, recommends an average of 14% personal debt, to a range of 10% to 20%. We strive for zero debt. Our subject "debtor" in this exercise is way over his head with 30% of his net monthly income paying down debt. His employer provides health benefits and a 401(K) plan. Our "debtor" is also committed to compounding debt payments and to saving.

5

Section 1

$MART MONEY MANAGEMENT
debt proof your life...

You can be... **Debt Free**

Setting up the Account Schedule and Monthly Allocation from your Worksheet: *Debts*

Monthly Allocation	Account Schedule Month Jan. Yr. ____	Date Due	Amount Due	Date Paid	Amount Paid	Deposits	Cash Cushion	Checking Acct. Bal.	% $
100.00	Savings	—	100.00						
1250.00	Citibank—mortgage	1/22	1250.00						
150.00	State Farm—auto ins.	2/9	150.00						
75.00	Met Life—insurance	1/20	75.00						
75.00	Verizon—telephone	2/8	82.50						
140.00	National Grid—elec & gas	1/19	130.50						
65.00	Time Warner—cable	1/15	65.00						
45.00	Exxon-Mobil—gas	2/4	45.00	*expenses*					
350.00	Bank of America—auto loan	1/15	**12,600.00**						9% 94.50
250.00	Citibank—home equity loan	2/5	**8,020.00**						9.75% 65.16
100.00	GM MasterCard	2/6	**4,020.00**						16.9% 56.62
75.00	American Express	2/7	**3,750.00**						12.5% 39.06
50.00	Capital One—Visa card	2/9	**2,200.00**						14.9% 27.32
50.00	MBNA—MasterCard	1/18	**1,972.00**						14.9% 24.49
50.00	Bank of America (2) Visa	2/6	**1,825.00**						12.9% 19.62
100.00	Sears	1/19	**580.00**						21% 10.15
100.00	Macy's	2/6	**345.00**	*debts*					22.5% 6.47
3025.00	**Monthly Allocation**		**35,312.00**				982.00	282.00	343.39
282.00	**Checking Account Balance**								
+ 3725.00	**Estimated Monthly Income**								
= 4007.00	**Available Funds**								
− 3025.00	**Monthly Allocation**								
= 982.00	**Cash Cushion**								

— monthly expenses $1900 —
— debt payments $1125 per month —

Monthly Debt Payments $1125.00 ÷ Net Monthly Income $3,725.00 = 30.26%.

Section 1

$MART MONEY MANAGEMENT
debt proof your life...

You can be... **Debt Free**

Adjust Expense Estimate to Actual Bill

When a bill arrives and it doesn't match your estimate for that expense, make a few easy corrections. Accuracy in the system keeps you in control of your spending in Cash Cushion.

- Take notice of the adjustment to Verizon's telephone bill. The estimate of $75.00 increased to $82.50. (page 8)
- Under Monthly Allocation insert the corrected amount to $82.50.
- Under Account Schedule show the adjustment minus (-) $7.50.
- Record $82.50 under Amount Due column.
- Treat National Grid similarly. The actual bill of $130.50 was lower than the estimated amount of $140.00. (page 8)
- Under Monthly Allocation insert the corrected amount of $130.50.
- Under Account Schedule show the adjustment plus (+) $9.50.
- Record $130.50 under Amount Due column.

Transaction Record Guidelines for Entries in our System and your Checkbook Register

Transaction Record	Your Checkbook Register	Debt Free System		
		Deposit	Cash Cushion	Checking Account Balance
1-bill payment listed under *accounts schedule*	x			x
2-deposit accounted for under *estimate monthly income*	x	x		x
3-debit card purchase	x		(-) x	(-) x
4-merchandise returned for credit-debit card	x		(+) x	(+) x
5-credit card purchase *(see transaction record illustrations 18-19*				
6-credit from adjusted bank statement	x		(+) x	(+) x
7-debit from adjusted bank statement	x		(-) x	(-) x
8-additional deposit *not* listed under *accounts schedule*	x	x	(+) x	(+) x
9-check paid for item *not* listed under *accounts schedule*	x		(-) x	(-) x
10-adjustments to allocations (+) (-)			x	
11-ATM withdrawal	x		(-) x	(-) x

Consider the following options: if you were to set-up two checking accounts with your bank, one for recurring expenses/debts, and one for miscellaneous cash spending to duplicate our Cash Cushion system, your objective would still not accomplish the simplicity and ease our formulas for cash control, debt management and credit card spending provide. There is no other system or method that can duplicate the Debt Free System, and no budgets are required!

The PCF Formula to a Debt Free Life:
Checking Account Balance + Estimated Monthly Income = Available Funds − Monthly Allocation = Cash Cushion

Section 1

$MART MONEY MANAGEMENT
debt proof your life...

You can be... **Debt Free**

Adjust Expense Estimate to Actual Bill

Monthly Allocation	Accounts Schedule Month _Jan._ Yr. _____	Date Due	Amount Due	Date Paid	Amount Paid	Deposits	Cash Cushion	Checking Acct. Bal.	% $
100.00	Savings	—	100.00	1/12	100.00				
1250.00	Citibank—mortgage	1/22	1250.00	1/17	1250.00				
150.00	State Farm—auto ins.	2/9	150.00	2/3	150.00				
75.00	Met Life—insurance	1/20	75.00	1/14	75.00				
<mark>82.50</mark> ~~75.00~~	<mark>adjust (−7.50)</mark> Verizon—telephone	2/8	82.50	2/2	82.50				
<mark>130.50</mark> ~~140.00~~	<mark>adjust (+9.50)</mark> National Grid—elec & gas	1/19	130.50	1/17	130.50				
65.00	Time Warner—cable	1/15	65.00	1/15	65.00				
45.00	Exxon-Mobil—gas	2/4	45.00	1/29	45.00				
350.00	Bank of America—auto loan	1/15	12,600.00	1/7	350.00				
250.00	Citibank—home equity loan	2/5	8,020.00	1/31	250.00				
100.00	GM MasterCard	2/6	4,020.00	1/31	100.00				
75.00	American Express	2/7	3,750.00	2/1	75.00				
50.00	Capital One—Visa card	2/9	2,200.00	2/4	50.00				
50.00	MBNA—MasterCard	1/18	1,972.00	1/11	50.00				
50.00	Bank of America—Visa card	2/6	1,825.00	2/1	50.00				
100.00	Sears	1/19	580.00	1/12	100.00				
100.00	Macy's	2/6	345.00	1/31	100.00				
3025.00	**Monthly Allocation**		35,312.00				982.00	282.00	
282.00	**Checking Account Balance**								
+ 3725.00	**Estimated Monthly Income**								
= 4007.00	**Available Funds**								
− 3025.00	**Monthly Allocation**								
= 982.00	**Cash Cushion**								

Section 1

$MART MONEY MANAGEMENT
debt proof your life...

You can be... **Debt Free**

❝*There is no dignity quite so impressive and no independence quite so important as living within your means.*❞

Annise Parker,
Mayor
Houston, Texas

❝*When you tap home equity to pay off bills, you kiss off those high monthly credit card payments, but you don't kiss off the debt. When debtors use home equity to pay off bills, they don't change their spending habits, and credit charges continue, driving the debtor deeper in debt on top of the home equity loan. Although the monthly payments are less, you end up paying more because the payments are stretched over a longer time period.*

Credit card companies can't foreclose on your home if you run into financial difficulties, but your home equity or cash-out refinancing are debts secured by your home. If you can't make payments, you can lose your home.

Debt paves the way to bankruptcy. Keep your cotton-picking paws off your nest egg.❞

Dorothy Rosen
Bankrate.com

Highlight Paid Bills – Take Control of Timely Payments
(worksheet illustration page 10)

As each bill is paid by check or online electronic bill pay, record entries in the Account Schedule and use a highlighter across the entire line of the paid bill. As you progress with bill payments, your attention will be drawn to the open, unpaid bills. Leave the current month's Account Schedule of your workbook manual open for daily review of unpaid Date Due bills. Stay on top of this schedule; protect your credit; you can negotiate a lower interest rate with on-time payments.

Section 1

$MART MONEY MANAGEMENT
debt proof your life...

You can be... **Debt Free**

Highlight Paid Bills – Taking Control of Timely Payments

Monthly Allocation	Accounts Schedule Month _Jan._ Yr. _____	Date Due	Amount Due	Date Paid	Amount Paid	Deposits	Cash Cushion	Checking Acct. Bal.	% $
100.00	Savings	—	100.00	1/12	100.00				
1250.00	Citibank—mortgage	1/22	1250.00	1/17	1250.00				
150.00	State Farm—auto ins.	2/9	150.00						
75.00	Met Life—insurance	1/20	75.00	1/14	75.00				
82.50 adjust (−7.50) 75.00	Verizon—telephone	2/8	82.50	2/2	82.50				
130.50 adjust (+9.50) 140.00	National Grid—elec & gas	1/19	130.50	1/17	130.50				
65.00	Time Warner—cable	1/15	65.00	1/15	65.00				
45.00	Exxon-Mobil—gas	2/4	45.00	1/29	45.00				
350.00	Bank of America—auto loan	1/15	12,600.00	1/7	350.00				9% 94.50
250.00	Citibank—home equity loan	2/5	8,200.00	1/31	250.00				9.75% 65.16
100.00	GM MasterCard	2/6	4,020.00						16.9% 56.62
75.00	American Express	2/7	3,750.00						12.5% 39.06
50.00	Capital One—Visa card	2/9	2,200.00						14.9% 27.32
50.00	MBNA—MasterCard	1/18	1,972.00	1/11	50.00				14.9% 24.49
50.00	Bank of America (2) Visa	2/6	1,825.00						12.9% 19.62
100.00	Sears	1/19	580.00	1/12	100.00				21% 10.15
100.00	Macy's	2/6	345.00						22.5% 6.47
3025.00	**Monthly Allocation**		35,312.00				982.00	282.00	343.39
282.00	**Checking Account Balance**								
+ 3725.00	**Estimated Monthly Income**								
= 4007.00	**Available Funds**								
− 3025.00	**Monthly Allocation**								
= 982.00	**Cash Cushion**								

$MART MONEY MANAGEMENT
debt proof your life...

Section 1

You can be... **Debt Free**

Freddy Frugal Says:
The Cornerstone to Living a Debt Free Life is Frugality.

If you follow our system and you are drawn down to making low or minimum payments on credit card debts in order to have enough for Cash Cushion spending, you have choices to make:

- Change your life style: be frugal.
- Sell or move to lower cost of housing.
- Trade out high cost auto payments for lower cost vehicles.
- Buy used instead of new big-ticket items: cars, furniture and appliances.
- Buy in thrift stores, such as Good Will, Salvation Army, for clothes and household items.
- Shop $1.00 stores for basic necessities.

Buy groceries with coupons. Look for sale items and cheaper store brands. Stock up on especially good buys. Shop with a list and stick to it.

Mediocrity vs. Excellence

Mediocrity is not all bad. It can come in the form of a hamburger. Consider thousands of fast food restaurants that serve hamburgers. That's *planned* mediocrity. *Excellence* comes in the form of innovative thinking in search of a product or service that will *exceed* all expectations. In its most natural form, *excellence* is driven by an *attitude* to be the very best. We strive for *excellence* in our Debt Free model.

January's Account Schedule and Monthly Allocation (worksheet illustration page 12)

Action column: % - $. TIA: Take Immediate Action to reduce debt and interest expense. Each debt has an interest rate posted in the % column. Under the $ sign are the amounts of finance charges, total for the month $343.39. Thousands of dollars are lost every year instead of saved and invested to build wealth. Call your credit card providers and negotiate a reduced interest rate. Ask them to cancel penalties, and eliminate late fees. Look for other card issuers for lower rates.

Change Your Life Style: Meet Freddy Frugal

There may be a neighbor of yours who lives down the block in a modest house in a typical working class neighborhood, has a good job, and drives a used Chevy pick-up truck. All of his household appliances, living room, dining room, and bedroom furniture were bought used, from second hand stores, and estate sales through classified newspaper ads. He invests 15% of his income adjusted every year through a mutual fund company. With automatic monthly transfers from his checking account, he systematically invests a fixed amount into a Roth Individual Retirement Account of stocks and bonds, low cost index funds, and exchange traded funds (ETF's) plus other securities. From all outward appearances, his life style is not much different from any of the dozen neighbors on the block. But you would never guess he is a "closet frugal millionaire." He doesn't consider himself rich. To him, wealth is no more than a lifeline to a secure financial worry-free life.

The PCF Formula

This Positive Cash Flow formula is the flow of money into and out of your life, and the road map to taking control of your finances. Set out now, follow it, and take no detours!

Checking Account Balance
+Estimated Monthly Income
=Available Funds
-Monthly Allocation
=Cash Cushion

Section 1

$MART MONEY MANAGEMENT
debt proof your life...

You can be... **Debt Free**

January's Allocation Schedule and Monthly Allocation –
Action Column % - $ TIA: Take Immediate Action To Reduce Debt and Interest Expense

Monthly Allocation	Accounts Schedule Month _Jan._ Yr. ____	Date Due	Amount Due	Date Paid	Amount Paid	Deposits	Cash Cushion	Checking Acct. Bal.	% $
100.00	Savings	—	100.00	1/12	100.00				
1250.00	Citibank—mortgage	1/22	1250.00	1/17	1250.00				
150.00	State Farm—auto ins.	2/9	150.00	2/3	150.00				
75.00	Met Life—insurance	1/20	75.00	1/14	75.00				
82.50 adjust (−7.50) ~~75.00~~	Verizon—telephone	2/8	82.50	2/2	82.50				
130.50 adjust (+9.50) ~~140.00~~	National Grid—elec & gas	1/19	130.50	1/17	130.50				
65.00	Time Warner—cable	1/15	65.00	1/15	65.00				
45.00	Exxon-Mobil—gas	2/4	45.00	1/29	45.00				
350.00	Bank of America—auto loan	1/15	12,600.00	1/7	350.00				9% 94.50
250.00	Citibank—home equity loan	2/5	8,020.00	1/31	250.00				9.75% 65.16
100.00	GM MasterCard	2/6	4,020.00	1/31	100.00				16.9% 56.62
75.00	American Express	2/7	3,750.00	2/1	75.00				12.5% 39.06
50.00	Capital One—Visa card	2/9	2,200.00	2/4	50.00				14.9% 27.32
50.00	MBNA—MasterCard	1/18	1,972.00	1/11	50.00				14.9% 24.49
50.00	Bank of America—Visa card	2/6	1,825.00	2/1	50.00				12.9% 19.62
100.00	Sears	1/19	580.00	1/12	100.00				21% 10.15
100.00	Macy's	2/6	345.00	1/31	100.00				22.5% 6.47
3025.00	**Monthly Allocation**		35,312.00				982.00	282.00	**343.39**
282.00	**Checking Account Balance**								
+ 3725.00	**Estimated Monthly Income**								
= 4007.00	**Available Funds**								
− 3025.00	**Monthly Allocation**								
= 982.00	**Cash Cushion**								

$MART MONEY MANAGEMENT
debt proof your life...

Section 2

You can be... Debt Free

Transaction Record is the same as your Checkbook Register, plus Cash Cushion (worksheet illustration page 14)

Bring forward January's Checking Account Balance ($282.00) from the Allocation Schedule to the Checking Account Balance in the Transaction Record.

- Carry forward the Cash Cushion balance ($982.00) to the Cash Cushion balance in the Transaction Record.
- **All expenses and debts listed under Monthly Allocation are deducted only from the Checking Account Balance.**
- All transaction entries charged to Cash Cushion, ATM withdrawals, debit card purchases, and adjustments are in bold figures.

The dashes under Cash Cushion and Checking Account Balance columns, draws your attention to the column *not* charged in the Transaction Record.

See page 7 Transaction Record Guidelines.

Adjust Expense Estimate in Cash Cushion Column

We want to keep Cash Cushion accurate for your spending needs. There could be a large swing in the estimate to the actual bill. Take the time to make these adjustments. This is how it works: Under Transaction Record, make a separate line entry for each adjustment of the estimate to the actual bill.

- **Adjust National Grid.** From the Allocation Schedule $140.00 was adjusted to $130.50. The adjustment of (+9.50) is recorded under the Amount Paid column.
- This amount of adjustment $9.50, is added to Cash Cushion, increasing the balance from $736.00 to $745.50. No other adjustment in Checking Account Balance is necessary since the adjustment affects Cash Cushion only.
- **Adjust Verizon** in the same manner. From the Allocation Schedule $75.00 was adjusted to $82.50, resulting in (-7.50) recorded under the Amount Paid column and deducted in Cash Cushion decreasing the balance from $384.50 to $377.14.
- Adjustments to Cash Cushion - besides keeping it accurate for our spending needs, it eliminates the need for budgets!

January's Transaction Record Balanced Bring Balance Forward to February (worksheet illustration page 15)

The system will balance. The Formula:
   Checking Account Balance $377.14
   -Less unpaid bills   .00
   =Cash Cushion $377.14

After the last bill is paid in the Account Schedule, the Cash Cushion and Checking Account Balance will match. It is not absolutely necessary to wait for the last bill to be paid to balance. There may be circumstances when you may want to start a new month before the last bill is paid. Just carry forward any unpaid bill to the next month's Allocation Schedule. Bring the balance forward to February.

We include the entire month of January's activity from Allocation to Transaction, to show how to stay in complete control of debt and spending.

- Check Account Schedule as each expense and debt was paid on time.
- Control cash with Cash Cushion: allocated $982.00, spent $604.86, balance $377.14
- Accuracy in details of cash management; the system balanced.

Section 2

$MART MONEY MANAGEMENT
debt proof your life...

You can be... **Debt Free**

Transaction Record is the same as your Checkbook Register + Cash Cushion. Adjust Expense Estimate in Cash Cushion Column

Credit Card Charge Bal.	Transaction Record Month Jan. Yr. _____	Date	Credit Card Charge	Date Paid	Amount Paid	Deposits	Cash Cushion	Checking Acct. Bal.	% $
	balance brought forward						982.00	282.00	
	Deposit—salary			1/3		745.00	—	1,027.00	
	MC debit—Price Chopper			1/5	46.20		**935.80**	980.80	
	ATM—withdrawal			1/5	100.00		**835.80**	880.80	
	MC debit—thrift store			1/6	37.00		**798.80**	843.80	
	Time Warner #378			1/7	65.00		—	778.80	
	Bk of America—auto loan #379			1/7	350.00		—	428.80	
	Deposit—salary			1/10		678.72	—	1,107.52	
	MC debit—Wal-Mart			1/10	62.80		**736.00**	1,044.72	
	MBNA #380			1/11	50.00		—	994.72	
	Sears #381			1/12	100.00		—	894.72	
	Savings			1/12	100.00		—	794.72	
	Met Life—insurance #382			1/14	75.00		—	719.72	
	Deposit—salary			1/17		745.00	—	1,464.72	
	Citibank—mortgage #383			1/17	1250.00		—	214.72	
	Adjust—National Grid			1/17	(+9.50)		**745.50**	—	
	National Grid #384			1/17	130.50		—	84.22	
	Deposit—salary			1/24		811.28	—	895.50	
	ATM—withdrawal			1/26	200.00		**545.50**	695.50	
	MC debit—Wal-Mart			1/26	92.50		**453.00**	603.00	
	MC credit—mds. ret'd. Wal-Mart			1/28		(+)16.80	**469.80**	619.80	
	Exxon-Mobil #385			1/29	45.00		—	574.80	
	Citibank—home equity loan #386			1/31	250.00		—	324.80	
	Deposit—salary			1/31		745.00	—	1,069.80	
	GM Mastercard #387			1/31	100.00		—	969.80	

Section 2

$MART MONEY MANAGEMENT
debt proof your life...

You can be... **Debt Free**

January's Transaction Record Balanced — Bring Balance Forward to February

Credit Card Charge Bal.	Transaction Record Month Jan. Yr. ___	Date	Credit Card Charge	Date Paid	Amount Paid	Deposits	Cash Cushion	Checking Acct. Bal.	% $
	balance brought forward ck #						469.80	969.80	
	Macy's #388			1/31	100.00		—	869.80	
	MC debit—Price Chopper			2/1	62.50		407.30	807.30	
	American Express #389			2/1	75.00		—	732.30	
	Bank of America (2) Visa #390			2/1	50.00		—	682.30	
	MC debit—Barnes & Noble			2/2	22.80		384.50	659.50	
	Adjust—Verizon			2/2	(−7.50)		377.00	—	
	Interest—checkbook register			2/2		(+).14	**377.14**	659.64	
	Verizon—telephone #391			2/2	82.50		—	577.14	
	State Farm—auto insurance #392			2/3	150.00		—	427.14	
	Capital One—Visa #393			2/4	50.00		—	**377.14**	

Section 2

$MART MONEY MANAGEMENT
debt proof your life...

You can be... **Debt Free**

Credit Card Charge Bal.	**Transaction Record** Month _____ Yr. _____	Date	Credit Card Charge	Date Paid	Amount Paid	Deposits	Cash Cushion	Checking Acct. Bal.	% $
	balance brought forward								

15-1

Section 2

$MART MONEY MANAGEMENT
debt proof your life...

You can be... **Debt Free**

Start Next Month's Allocation Schedule – February
(worksheet illustration page 17)

- Carry forward January's Checking Account Balance $377.14.
- Complete February's Allocation Schedule and Monthly Allocation:

Checking Account Balance	377.14
+Estimated Monthly Income	3,800.00
=Available Funds	4,177.14
-Monthly Allocation	3,135.00
=Cash Cushion	1,042.14

February's Completed Allocation Schedule
(worksheet illustration page 17)

- Study February's completed Allocation Schedule.
- Each expense and debt paid on time.
- Debt reduced with no increase in spending:

January	35,312.00
February	34,530.39
Reduction	781.61

- Finance charges reduced:

January	343.39
February	334.73
Reduction	8.66

- Savings increased to 200.00.

"*With the **CREDIT CARD REFORM ACT** February 2010, approximately 180 million Americans will see something new when they review their credit card statement - A full disclosure of their payoff time:*

How long it will take to pay their credit card balance in full if making only minimum payments. The total amount they will pay, including interest, if they make only minimum payments. How much they need to pay off the balance in 36 months.

*Intended to establish fair and transparent practices, the **CREDIT CARD REFORM ACT** is one of a number of regulatory changes aimed at providing consumers with better information so they can make more educated borrowing decisions.*"

Anthony Lanzillo
Senior Vice President
Key Bank:
The above was taken in part, from an article written for **The Spotlight Weekly** Newspaper, Delmar, NY.

Section 2

$MART MONEY MANAGEMENT
debt proof your life...

You can be... **Debt Free**

February's Account Schedule: Debt and Finance Charges Reduced-Savings Increased

Monthly Allocation	Account Schedule Month Feb. Yr. ____	Date Due	Amount Due	Date Paid	Amount Paid	Deposits	Cash Cushion	Checking Acct. Bal.	% $
200.00	Savings	—	200.00	3/5	200.00				
1250.00	Citibank—mortgage	2/22	1250.00	2/16	1250.00				
150.00	State Farm—auto ins.	3/9	150.00	3/5	150.00				
75.00	Met Life—insurance	2/20	75.00	2/16	75.00				
79.10 adjust (+5.90) ~~85.00~~	Verizon—telephone	3/6	79.10	3/5	79.10				
112.60 adjust (+12.40) ~~125.00~~	National Grid—elec & gas	2/16	112.60	2/10	112.60				
65.00	Time Warner—cable	2/12	65.00	2/6	65.00				
57.80 adjust (+2.20) ~~60.00~~	Exxon-Mobil—gas	3/2	57.80	2/22	57.80				
350.00	Bank of America—auto loan	2/15	12,344.50	2/9	350.00				9% 92.58
250.00	Citibank—home equity loan	3/5	7,835.16	3/2	250.00				9.75% 63.66
100.00	GM MasterCard	3/6	3,976.62	3/2	100.00				16.9% 56.00
75.00	American Express	3/8	3,714.06	3/5	75.00				12.5% 38.69
50.00	Capital One—Visa card	3/10	2,177.32	3/2	50.00				14.9% 27.04
50.00	MBNA—MasterCard	2/18	1,946.49	2/14	50.00				14.9% 24.17
50.00	Bank of America—Visa card	3/8	1,794.62	3/5	50.00				12.9% 19.29
100.00	Sears	2/19	490.15	2/15	100.00				21% 8.58
100.00	Macy's	3/5	251.47	3/1	100.00				22.5% 4.72
3,135.00	**Monthly Allocation**		34,530.39				1042.14	377.14	**334.73**
377.14	**Checking Account Balance**								
+ 3,800.00	**Estimated Monthly Income**								
= 4,177.14	**Available Funds**								
− 3,135.00	**Monthly Allocation**								
= 1042.14	**Cash Cushion**								

Section 2

$MART MONEY MANAGEMENT
debt proof your life...

You can be... **Debt Free**

The Vision

A goal is a stated objective. A vision is a picture of that goal. So, if wealth is the number of years you can live comfortably without working, what's your vision? Goals are often lost because you have no real control of the future. But you can hold the vision firmly in your mind, and let it sustain your efforts to stay in control of your spending and debts. Unaltered by time and circumstance the vision remains the same.

Success Lies Somewhere Between Obsession and Passion

As a personal debt counselor, private practitioner and instructor of Debt Free at Community & Professional Education, Hudson Valley Community College, Troy NY, we have observed on occasion, an unusual phenomenon in some of our clients and students - the power of obsessive determination to change from debt driven spenders to frugal managers in complete control of their money and their lives. Once success was achieved, the obsessive behavior was replaced by every day habits of frugality driven by the passion to stay debt free, save and accumulate wealth.

Transaction Record Guidelines for Credit Card Charges (worksheet illustration page 19)

Since the publication of our Debt Free System in 2004, we modified our work-study manual. The system remains the same. However, for those clients who are debt free, we have integrated into our system, credit card charges. Our recommendation is to use only a debit card. Use of a credit card for some folks is a black-hole debt-trap. If you choose to spend with credit cards, you will need controls. Know how much you spend, don't carry a debt balance; pay in full each month. *There are no provisions in our system for credit card spending beyond the balance in the Cash Cushion column.*

- Enter each credit card purchase in Credit Card Charge column.
- Reduce the balance in Cash Cushion for each amount of credit card charge.
- Add each credit card charge to the Credit Card Charge Balance.

Debt Management is not a Science. There may be hundreds of knowledgeable debt management practitioners, writers, counselors and advisors with a variety of methods that can help you achieve financial independence. Our Mission and Purpose, is a simple no budget, cash control, zero debt management system.

Simple vs. Complex. At our educational workshops, our students, and clients from our private practice, will on occasion, express an opinion or challenge one of our long held concepts of debt management. Example: balancing the checkbook. We never thought that balancing a checkbook by reconciling the bank statement was a complex procedure. We discovered that some of our students who use electronic online banking, download their account bank statement, and use it as their own checkbook balance, avoiding balancing their checkbook. At one of our workshops, a student blurted out, "go paperless dude." I assumed that since a paper statement no longer comes in the mail, the students adjusted their checkbooks with the down loaded bank statements. I have since learned by e-mail messages from former students that the online banking statement replaced the checkbook register entirely, and in its place the Debt Free Monthly Account Schedule and Transaction Record became the primary method of financial control! Don't equate simplicity with unsophisticated thinking.

A word of caution: use the Transaction Record just as you would use your checkbook register. Make entries daily, maintain balances and reconcile with a paper or online electronic down-loaded bank statement.

Balance Transaction Record and Credit Card Charge Balance (worksheet illustration page 20)

February's Checking Account Balance $862.64 less Credit Card Charge Balance of $458.60 will show a balance of $404.04 matching the balance of $404.04 in Cash Cushion.

Section 2

$MART MONEY MANAGEMENT
debt proof your life...

You can be... **Debt Free**

Transaction Record Guidelines for Credit Card Charges: Credit Card Charges Column List Credit Charges Credit Card Charge Balance Column add (+) Each Charge to Balance. Cash Cushion Column Deduct (-) Credit Card Charges from Balance

Credit Card Charge Bal.	**Transaction Record** Month _Feb._ Yr. ___	Date	Credit Card Charge	Date Paid	Amount Paid	Deposits	Cash Cushion	Checking Acct. Bal.	% $
	balance brought forward						1042.14	377.14	
	Deposit—salary			2/1		760.26	—	1,137.40	
45.70	Wal-mart Bk of America—Visa cr. chg.	2/2	45.70				996.44	—	
118.20	CVS Bk of America—Visa cr. chg.	2/4	72.50				923.94	—	
	e-bill pay Time Warner			2/6	65.00		—	1,072.40	
	Deposit—salary			2/7		760.00	—	1,832.40	
	e-bill pay Bk of America—auto loan			2/9	350.00		—	1,482.40	
	ATM—withdrawal Bk of America			2/9	200.00		723.94	1,282.40	
	e-bill pay National Grid			2/10	112.60		—	1,169.80	
	Adjust—National Grid			2/10	(+12.40)		736.34	—	
205.35	Wal-mart Bk of America—Visa cr. chg.	2/10	87.15				649.19	—	
	e-bill pay MBNA—Mastercard			2/14	50.00		—	1,119.80	
	Deposit—salary			2/14		690.40	—	1,810.20	
	e-bill pay Sears			2/15	100.00		—	1,710.20	
	e-bill pay Met-Life Insurance			2/16	75.00		—	1,635.20	
	e-bill pay Citibank—mortgage			2/16	1,250.00		—	385.20	
	Deposit—salary			2/21		716.14	—	1,101.34	
241.60	Good-will Bk of America—Visa cr. chg.	2/22	36.25				612.94	—	
	e-bill pay Exxon-Mobil—gas			2/22	57.80		—	1,043.54	
	Adjust—Exxon-Mobil			2/22	(+2.20)		615.14	—	
331.80	Wal-mart Bk of America—Visa cr. chg.	2/23	90.20				524.94	—	
	Deposit—salary			2/28		873.20	—	1,916.74	
	e-bill pay Macy's			3/1	100.00		—	1,816.74	
	e-bill pay Citibank—Home Equity loan			3/2	250.00		—	1,566.74	

Section 2

$MART MONEY MANAGEMENT
debt proof your life...

You can be... **Debt Free**

Balancing Transaction Record and Credit Card Charge Balance

Credit Card Charge Bal.	Transaction Record Month Feb. Yr. ____	Date	Credit Card Charge	Date Paid	Amount Paid	Deposits	Cash Cushion	Checking Acct. Bal.	% $
331.80	balance brought forward						524.94	1,566.74	
	e-bill pay GM Mastercard			3/2	100.00		—	1,466.74	
	e-bill pay Bk of America—Visa			3/5	50.00		—	1,416.74	
	e-bill pay American Express			3/5	75.00		—	1,341.74	
458.60	CVS Bk of America—Visa cr. chg.	3/6	126.80				398.14	—	
	e-bill pay State Farm			3/5	150.00		—	1,191.74	
	e-bill pay Verizon			3/5	79.10		—	1,112.64	
	Adjust—Verizon			3/5	(+5.90)		404.04	—	
	e-bill pay Capital One Visa Card			3/5	50.00		—	1,062.64	
	Savings			3/5	200.00		—	862.64	
458.60							**404.04**	**862.64**	
	Checking Acct. Bal							862.64	
−	Less unpaid invoices							− 0 −	
−	Credit card charges							458.60	
=	Cash Cushion							404.04	

20

Section 3

$MART MONEY MANAGEMENT
debt proof your life...

You can be... **Debt Free**

Learn the best kept secret:
The power of compound interest

You should be aware of the effect of compound interest on debt and savings. If you are on the wrong side of that compound interest, with high credit card interest rates, it can take years to pay off the debt. By accelerating debt payments, you reverse the cycle. Compounding is cutting finance charges as well as reducing debt. There is a saying about compounding: "Those who understand it earn it, those who don't pay it."

Compounding debt payments

Expenses are your operating costs: overhead in maintaining your home and all the daily activities. Some expenses are variable; telephone, gas & electric etc; but other expenses like rent/mortgage, insurance, are relatively fixed. In our Monthly Allocation, expenses are $1900 per month, debt payments are $1125 per month. Total Monthly Allocation is $3025. Essentially, the Monthly Allocation of $3025 stays intact except for the variable expenses. Now let's get started with compounding. When listing your debts, start with the largest amount owed, and process down to the smallest balance owed.

Make the largest payment amount $100 to the smallest debt balance, Macy's $345. Once Macy's debt is paid in full, add Macy's $100 payment to the next smaller debt, Sears $545. Sears' payment now will be $200. As you continue paying all debts every month, you will be adding each paid in full debt payment on to the next debt. The monthly payment of $1125 per month remains the same until all debts are paid in full. This is compounding.

The high cost of single debt reduction payments

In single debt reduction, after the first debt is paid off, Macy's $345, the next monthly debt payments are reduced by the amount of that debt payment. Example: the starting monthly debt payments total $1125. After Macy's debt payment of $100 per month is paid in full, next month's allocation of debt payments would be $1025. By following this method, after Sears' debt payment of $100 per month is paid in full, it reduces the next month's allocation to $925. See the chart below for the penalty of single debt reduction.

Summary of Payment Methods: Single Debt Reduction vs. Compounded Payments

Debts	Debt Balance	Monthly Payment	Finance Rate	Without Compounding		With Compounding	
				Number of Payments	Total Payments	Number of Payments	Total Payments
Bank of America	12,600.00	350.00	9.00%	43	14,741.00	38	14,701.96
Citibank	8,020.00	250.00	9.75	38	9,329.73	36	9,324.56
GM MasterCard	4,020.00	100.00	16.90	60	5,971.19	35	5,505.96
American Express	3,750.00	75.00	12.50	71	5,324.63	30	4,658.85
Capital One	2,200.00	50.00	14.90	65	3,202.52	23	2,704.77
MBNA MasterCard	1,972.00	50.00	14.90	55	2,726.05	18	2,310.83
Bank of America (2)	1,825.00	50.00	12.90	47	2,329.69	12	1,990.11
Sears	580.00	100.00	21.00	7	617.05	5	614.05
Macy's	345.00	100.00	22.50	4	360.22	4	360.22
Totals	35,312.00	1,125.00		71	44,602.72	38 months	42,171.31

If you used single debt reduction, you would have paid the entire debt in 5 years and 11 months, at a cost of $44,602.72. By using our method of accelerated debt payments, compounding would have paid off the entire debt in 3 years and 2 months, in nearly half the time, at a cost of $42,171.31, a savings of $2,431.41. We use this chart as an illustration of good debt management.

Section 3

$MART MONEY MANAGEMENT
debt proof your life...

You can be... **Debt Free**

Hammer the Debt-Accelerated Debt Payment Plan = Compounding

By accelerating debt payments, compounding is cutting finance charges as well as reducing debt. Payments of $1125. per month, until all debts are paid, is the compounding factor. All payments in remaining balance, include interest charges. Compounding cuts finance charges as well as time in debt.

Year 1: See how payments starting with Macy's $100 compounds: from the smallest debt $345. to the largest debt $12,600., BOA

	*12600.	8020.	4020.	3750.	2200.	1972.	1825.	580.	345.	Monthly	Remaining
Month	BOA	Citibank	GM MC	AMEX	Capital One	MBNA MC	BOA-2	Sears	Macy's	Payment	Balance
1	350.00	250.00	100.00	75.00	50.00	50.00	50.00	100.00	100.00	1,125.	34,530.39
2	350.00	250.00	100.00	75.00	50.00	50.00	50.00	100.00	100.00	1,125.	33,740.11
3	350.00	250.00	100.00	75.00	50.00	50.00	50.00	100.00	100.00	1,125.	32,941.07
4	350.00	250.00	100.00	75.00	50.00	50.00	50.00	139.78	60.22	1,125.	32,133.15
5	350.00	250.00	100.00	75.00	50.00	50.00	75.73	174.27	0.00	1,125.	31,316.29
6	350.00	250.00	100.00	75.00	50.00	50.00	250.00	0.00	0.00	1,125.	30,490.63
7	350.00	250.00	100.00	75.00	50.00	50.00	250.00	0.00	0.00	1,125.	29,657.23
8	350.00	250.00	100.00	75.00	50.00	50.00	250.00	0.00	0.00	1,125.	28,816.01
9	350.00	250.00	100.00	75.00	50.00	50.00	250.00	0.00	0.00	1,125.	27,966.91
10	350.00	250.00	100.00	75.00	50.00	50.00	250.00	0.00	0.00	1,125.	27,109.85
11	350.00	250.00	100.00	75.00	50.00	50.00	250.00	0.00	0.00	1,125.	26,244.74
12	350.00	250.00	100.00	75.00	50.00	85.62	214.38	0.00	0.00	1,125.	25,371.50

Year 2: accelerated debt payment plan: 1125.00 per month compounds:

Month	BOA	Citibank	GM MC	AMEX	Capital One	MBNA MC	BOA-2	Sears	Macy's	Monthly Payment	Remaining Balance
1	350.00	250.00	100.00	75.00	50.00	300.00	0.00	0.00	0.00	1,125.	24,490.01
2	350.00	250.00	100.00	75.00	50.00	300.00	0.00	0.00	0.00	1,125.	23,599.81
3	350.00	250.00	100.00	75.00	50.00	300.00	0.00	0.00	0.00	1,125.	22,700.82
4	350.00	250.00	100.00	75.00	50.00	300.00	0.00	0.00	0.00	1,125.	21,792.95
5	350.00	250.00	100.00	75.00	50.00	300.00	0.00	0.00	0.00	1,125.	20,876.10
6	350.00	250.00	100.00	75.00	174.79	175.21	0.00	0.00	0.00	1,125.	19,950.17
7	350.00	250.00	100.00	75.00	350.00	0.00	0.00	0.00	0.00	1,125.	19,015.09
8	350.00	250.00	100.00	75.00	350.00	0.00	0.00	0.00	0.00	1,125.	18,070.74
9	350.00	250.00	100.00	75.00	350.00	0.00	0.00	0.00	0.00	1,125.	17,117.03
10	350.00	250.00	100.00	75.00	350.00	0.00	0.00	0.00	0.00	1,125.	16,153.86
11	350.00	250.00	100.00	145.02	279.98	0.00	0.00	0.00	0.00	1,125.	15,181.14
12	350.00	250.00	100.00	425.00	0.00	0.00	0.00	0.00	0.00	1,125.	14,198.89

Year 3: accelerated debt payment plan compounds:

Month	BOA	Citibank	GM MC	AMEX	Capital One	MBNA MC	BOA-2	Sears	Macy's	Monthly Payment	Remaining Balance
1	350.00	250.00	100.00	425.00	0.00	0.00	0.00	0.00	0.00	1,125.	13,207.59
2	350.00	250.00	100.00	425.00	0.00	0.00	0.00	0.00	0.00	1,125.	12,207.15
3	350.00	250.00	100.00	425.00	0.00	0.00	0.00	0.00	0.00	1,125.	11,197.48
4	350.00	250.00	100.00	425.00	0.00	0.00	0.00	0.00	0.00	1,125.	10,178.49
5	350.00	250.00	100.00	425.00	0.00	0.00	0.00	0.00	0.00	1,125.	9,150.10
6	350.00	250.00	211.17	313.83	0.00	0.00	0.00	0.00	0.00	1,125.	8,112.20
7	350.00	250.00	525.00	0.00	0.00	0.00	0.00	0.00	0.00	1,125.	7,064.31
8	350.00	250.00	525.00	0.00	0.00	0.00	0.00	0.00	0.00	1,125.	6,005.17
9	350.00	250.00	525.00	0.00	0.00	0.00	0.00	0.00	0.00	1,125.	4,934.65
10	350.00	250.00	525.00	0.00	0.00	0.00	0.00	0.00	0.00	1,125.	3,852.61
11	350.00	480.21	294.79	0.00	0.00	0.00	0.00	0.00	0.00	1,125.	2,758.93
12	780.65	344.35	0.00	0.00	0.00	0.00	0.00	0.00	0.00	1,125.	1,654.83

Year 4: accelerated debt payment plan, 1,125 per month, paid in full: 35,312 paid in 3 years and 2 months

Month	BOA	Citibank	GM MC	AMEX	Capital One	MBNA MC	BOA-2	Sears	Macy's	Monthly Payment	Remaining Balance
1	1125.00	0.00	0.00	0.00	0.00	0.00	0.00	0.00	0.00	1,125.	542.24
2	546.31	0.00	0.00	0.00	0.00	0.00	0.00	0.00	0.00	546.31	0.00

*Starting debt balance for each account.

$MART MONEY MANAGEMENT
debt proof your life...

Section 3

You can be... **Debt Free**

Debt Free is Your Bridge Between Substance and Style

Will it be style to impress others and a continuation of debt? Or will it be a solid financial structure; a home which fits comfortably within your income level; a used car purchased with 30,000 miles that now has 130,000 on it. Individual Retirement Account and a 401(K) Plan you maximize each year; College Savings Plan #529 tax deferred and exempt for your children's education; Disability Insurance to protect your family if you are disabled; Health Insurance; should you lose your job, COBRA, your employer sponsored health insurance coverage; Term life insurance for added protection for your family in the event of your death; Long Term Health Care for your old age; wealth accumulation for retirement; Substance! How sweet it is!

Bill Paying Process – Master the Paper Trail

You can't take control of your debts unless you control the paper trail. Even if you use online electronic bill pay, you create a printed copy that requires filing. Questions: what do you do with debit/credit card receipts? Where do you keep your unpaid bills? Where do you file paid bills? Do you use the blank reconciliation form on the back of the bank statement to balance your checkbook?

The Envelope: Debit/Credit Card Receipts

When you make a debit/credit card purchase, place the receipts in your wallet. Each evening, pull out the receipts, and across the top of each receipt write the date, card name and amount. This will eliminate the need to search again for dates and amounts. On 3x5 envelopes mark as follows:

- Debit/Credit Card Bank Name
- ATM Withdrawal/Bank Name
- Deposits/Bank Name
- Gas Card/Company Name
- Cash Receipts
- Save cash receipts for purchases you may want to return for credit
- For paid bills use a file box or letter size folders. Name the file. Store and identify all information in the folder: insurance, utilities etc. Mark one folder for unpaid bills.
- Check the Account Schedule each evening for timely payments.

Balance your Checkbook

There isn't a standard configuration that banks use for reconciling the bank statement and balancing the checkbook register. Here is a simple approach; just follow the steps:

1- Ending balance bank statement ....$ _____
2- Add deposits/credits not listed on bank statement   _____
3- Subtotal 1 & 2 ....$ _____
4- List checks outstanding from your checkbook:

$ _____
_____
_____

5- Total outstanding checks $ _____ $ _____
6- Substract 5-3 $ _____
7- Ending checkbook balance $ _____

23

$MART MONEY MANAGEMENT
debt proof your life...

You can be... **Debt Free**

The American Dream Part 1

Retirement is not built on debt, consumption or increasing value of home ownership, but on savings and investments. Houses should be regarded as a place to live, not as an appreciating retirement fund.

Years ago, your parents bought a home with a 20% down payment, accumulated from savings over a number of years. Your father was the sole wage earner, while your mother took care of you and the home. Your Mom and Dad paid for your college education. After you left and went on your own, your mother worked, and saved most of her income for retirement.

The bank loan officer required a down payment commensurate with one wage earners capacity to pay the mortgage, credit history, and loan-to-value of the property. At the end of the day, consumers had to have a history of making timely payments and the ability to repay and not have too much of their income being applied to debt, also known as debt-to-income ratio. The loan officer serviced the mortgage loan, as it remained with the bank. Prudence was the character of the time, for the borrower and the lender.

What happened in the years since borrowers and lenders played out their roles in a prudent manner, and lived like Freddy Frugal? The fact is, too many householders are dependent on two paychecks to meet mortgage payments and without enough savings the loss of one paycheck can cause a default, especially if the mortgage has an adjustable rate. In this current housing market the mortgage is upside down, you owe more than the house is worth. You bought it with the expectation of appreciating house values, so you could flip it for a profit, or upgrade it to a larger home. Pure speculation!

Your home is your shelter. It does not replace the need to save money for retirement. Even with the advantage of tax deductions for mortgage interest and property taxes, the advantage can be offset by declining home values, increasing adjustable rate mortgages, leveraged financing, and consumer debt.

There are rentals that provide a wide range of moderate prices. People can get more house for the money, and have the ability to save. Consider the suggestions on Page 23:

The Bridge Between Substance (financial security) and Your Life Style

- Savings
- 401(K)
- Roth Individual Retirement Account
- Health Insurance
- Disability insurance
- Term life insurance
- Long term health care
- College Saving Plan #529
- Annuities
- Wealth accumulation

If renting can allow you to bridge the gap, to gain all the advantages of financial security, against the loss of this security because of the cost of home ownership, how would *you* evaluate this dilemma?

Owning a home is fine if you have the substance to go along with home ownership. After retirement you can sell your house for a smaller home without a mortgage. With long term savings and investments, you can live on social security, retirement income from interest on investments, and still maintain the principal. You will have lived just like Freddy Frugal, "the closet frugal millionaire."

Section 4

$MART MONEY MANAGEMENT
debt proof your life...

You can be... **Debt Free**

American Dream Part 2

The children in this American Dream saga, wanted to create a comfortable retirement situation for their ageing parents, in appreciation for the life-training examples of generosity; and at the same time frugality; common sense decision making; and the love they shared for each other. His dad was a carpenter, painter, and sometimes auto mechanic, and when construction work slowed down, he developed a "handyman" reputation, and always found work to support his family.

Not far from where his parents lived, Joseph the son, found a nice two bedroom, bath and a half condominium in a cul-de-sac neighborhood for sale. Joseph discussed this with his parents and once they saw the condo they eagerly agreed to Joseph's plan:

- Joseph purchases the condo for $125,000, plus improvements, $28,400, investing $153,400.
- His mom and dad sold their home for $166,800 and moved into the condo. Dad wrote a check to his son for $153,400.
- Joseph signed a note and mortgage to his father and mother for $153,400 at 5.75% for 20 years.
- Joseph's father is now a note and mortgage holder, and receives a monthly check for the mortgage of $1077.
- Joseph's father is also a renter, and sends a check to his son for rent, $1077.
- Joseph deducts the condo's mortgage interest, property taxes and maintenance fees from his federal taxes in the amount of $6500.
- Joseph's mother and father live comfortably in retirement from interest income of investments, without having to draw down the principal, and additional savings of $6500 a year in living expenses.

> **Additional Benefits**
>
> It was agreed between father and son, not to record the mortgage:
> Recording fees   70.00
> Mortgage recording tax <u>1892.00</u>
> Additional savings of   1962.00
>
> Joseph's lawyer draws up a contract, note and mortgage for all to sign.
>
> Joseph also gets to deduct depreciation of the $153,400 paid for the unit.
>
> Joseph's mother and father save $6500.00 in monthly housing costs, but pay only on the interest income of the note
>   (which declines over time).

Section 5

$MART MONEY MANAGEMENT
debt proof your life...

You can be... **Debt Free**

Wealth Accumulation: The source of wealth accumulation is the [1]systematic monthly investing a fixed amount; with [2]dollar cost averaging, and the [3]compounding of interest; in [4]low cost, [5]diversified mutual funds; in [6]tax free Individual Retirement Account over a period of [7]many years.

The following chart will reveal the secret of wealth accumulation by compounding, and automatic monthly transfers from checking into an IRA account

Your starting balance	2500.	Future value	19,112.16	
Annual rate of return	9%	Total interest	4,612.16	
Monthly contribution	200.	Total contribution	12,000.	First step get out of debt.
Number of years	5			
				1-Systematic monthly investing of a
Your starting balance	2500.	Future value	45,121.49	fixed amount automatically
Annual rate of return	9%	Total interest	18,621.49	transferred from checking to
Monthly contribution	200.	Total contribution	24,000.	an Individual Retirement
Number of years	10			Account.
				2- Dollar cost averaging. As the
Your starting balance	2500.	Future value	85,843.87	stock market moves up and
Annual rate of return	9%	Total interest	47,343.87	down, you buy more shares when
Monthly contribution	200.	Total contribution	36,000.	the price drops, and fewer shares
Number of years	15			when the price rises.
				3-Compounding of interest as
Your starting balance	2500.	Future value	149,602.00	shown in this chart.
Annual rate of return	9%	Total interest	99,102.08	
Monthly contribution	200.	Total contribution	48,000.	
Number of years	20			
				4- Low cost. Just as returns
Your starting balance	2500.	Future value	249,427.07	(interest) compounds, so do
Annual rate of return	9%	Total interest	186,927.07	costs. Invest in Exchange Traded Funds,
Monthly contribution	200.	Total contribution	60,000.	Index Funds, and low cost Mutual Funds.
Number of years	25			
				5-Reduce risk with diversification.
Your starting balance	2500.	Future value	405,721.20	U.S bonds, stocks, money
Annual rate of return	9%	Total interest	331,221.20	market funds. International
Monthly contribution	200.	Total contribution	72,000.	stocks and bonds.
Number of years	30			
				6-Tax Free IRA: Invest in a Roth
Your starting balance	2500.	Future value	650,427.92	IRA, after tax investing, tax free
Annual rate of return	9%	Total interest	563.927.92	on withdrawal.
Monthly contribution	200.	Total contribution	84,000.	
Number of years	35			
				7-Long term outlook: Simplicity
Your starting balance	2500.	Future value	1,033,560.65	is the key. Avoid market time-
Annual rate of return	9%	Total interest	935,060.65	ing. In the long run you'll
Monthly contribution	200.	Total Contribution	96,000.	earn more.
Number of years	40			

Focus on simple planning rules that have proven results over many years of investing. Don't invest money you can't afford to lose. Don't let excessive fees eat into your returns. Diversify investments; read, study, learn about low cost mutual and index funds. The real secret to growing wealth is the systematic transfer of a fixed amount from your checking account automatically every month, into your individual retirement account. Pay yourself first. Listen to Freddy Frugal the closet frugal millionaire.